WELTANSCHAUUNG, SCIENCE AND ECONOMY

From a testimonial volume in honor of the sixtieth birthday of Hjalmar Schacht.

WERNER SOMBART

WELTANSCHAUUNG SCIENCE AND ECONOMY

Translated by
PHILIP JOHNSON

NEW YORK
VERITAS PRESS
1939

TRANSLATOR'S PREFACE

THE German title of this book is *Weltanschauung, Wissenschaft und Wirtschaft*.

The word *Weltanschauung* I have retained in the translation since I feel that it has already become a familiar term to English and American readers.

The word *Wissenschaft* I have translated "science." But the German word corresponds only to the broadest sense of the English word. The usual meaning of "science," as the equivalent of "natural science," is expressed by the German word *Naturwissenschaft*. Sciences, such as sociology, history, economics, *et al.*, which are not "natural sciences," are expressed in German by the words *Geisteswissenschaft* and *Kulturwissenschaft*. These terms I have translated "spiritual science" and "cultural science."

The word *Wirtschaft* I have translated "economy." The word denotes all economic activity. The word "economics" I have used to translate *Nationalökonomie*, that is, the science of economics as contrasted to economic activity.

For their kind help in the preparation of this translation, I wish to thank Professor Götz Briefs of George Washington University, Mr. Oskar Piest of the Veritas Press, Mr. Lawrence Dennis, author of *Is Capitalism Doomed?*, and most especially, for his thorough supervision, Professor Karl F. Geiser of Oberlin College, the translator of Sombart's *Deutscher Sozialismus,* who has now in preparation a translation of Sombart's *magnum opus, Der moderne Kapitalismus.*

PHILIP JOHNSON

NEW LONDON, O.
JULY, 1939

TABLE OF CONTENTS

ix

WELTANSCHAUUNG, SCIENCE AND
ECONOMY

INTRODUCTION

"Drei Worte nenn' ich Euch, schicksalschwer,
Sie gehen von Munde zu Munde."

"Three words I name to you, destiny laden,
They go from mouth to mouth."

THESE three words, singly and above all relative to each other, are the subject of discussion in all classes of society and by men of all shades of education: by the educated, by the uneducated, and worst of all by the half-educated. The three words are Weltanschauung — Science — Economy. These words and their relation to each other form the subject matter of this essay.

At once, therefore, I shall specify what I mean by each of them. For in common usage they have so many meanings that, unless I define them now, the argument will become confused.

Weltanschauung I call the totality of our interpretations of the world and of our life in the world (a problem of knowledge) ; also, it is the totality of the values by which we live (a problem of will) .

Weltanschauung is concerned with the decision of ultimate questions, with universal and general de-

3

cisions. The religious, political, epistemological or moral attitude of an individual is only a part of his Weltanschauung.

Science I call that mode of cognition which seeks to establish a universally valid body of knowledge, arranged in systematic order. Science is a unique, historical phenomenon, which exists only in Western civilization and only in "modern" times.

Science has the following characteristics:

1. The *secularization* of knowledge. The foundation, the purpose and the subject matter of knowledge (and the way it is understood) have been secularized.

The basis of knowledge has been secularized, in that it has changed from revelation to reason and experience. The purpose of knowledge has been secularized, in that we no longer seek knowledge for the sake of other-worldly values, but for the sake of earthly values (whether they be theoretical or practical). The subject matter of knowledge has been secularized, in that we seek today knowledge of things in their diversity, governed only by their own particular laws, dissolved out of the metaphysical context in which we had formerly conceived them.

2. The *differentiation* of the fields of knowledge. The different sections of the world are studied separately and become the subject matter of a separate science, or of a branch of a science.

3. The *democratization* of knowledge. Philoso-

phy, the elder sister of science, appeals only to the circle of the like-minded, to disciples; but science appeals "to all," to the undifferentiated mass of thinking beings. In contradistinction to philosophy, science, and this is its most important characteristic, strives for the universal validity of its conclusions, which should not be confused with their popular comprehensibility. And universal validity requires universal transmissibility as well; that is, scientific conclusions must be capable of being made completely objective, completely divorced from the personality of the knower. They must be "demonstrable," provable beyond the possibility of doubt.[1]

Economy I call that field of human culture that has to do with providing sustenance for man; that is, the supplying of material things.

All economy consists of the following parts:

1. The economic attitude (*Wirtschaftsgesinnung*) : the underlying purposes, motives, and rules of conduct which determine man's economic activity.

2. The economic order (*Ordnung*) : the objective norms and standards which govern all economy. These standards are the legal order, the conventional order and the moral order.

3. Technic: the means which men use to reach their economic goal.[2]

---

[1] A detailed discussion can be found in my book: *Die Drei Nationalökonomien,* 1930, chap. 7.

[2] A detailed discussion can be found in my book: *Die Ordnung des Wirtschaftslebens,* 2nd ed., 1927.

INTRODUCTION

In this essay I shall attempt to answer this question: Are these three concepts in any way "relative" to, or "dependent" on, each other? If so in what way? In a real, or an ideal, sense; in an accidental, or a necessary sense?

If we express the relation of our three concepts to each other by means of the copulative "and," three combinations are possible:

> Weltanschauung and economy
> Weltanschauung and science
> Science and economy.

As the reader will see, I have divided the essay into three chapters, each of which bears one of these titles.

CHAPTER ONE

WELTANSCHAUUNG AND ECONOMY

I. False Theories

IT is obvious that Weltanschauung and economy are very closely related and at no period in which men have thought about the two concepts, has there been any doubt about it. Indeed, in the nineteenth century this relation became the central problem of the historians. Primarily under the influence of Marxism, the conception arose that Weltanschauung was necessarily connected to economy; Weltanschauung was determined by economy; economy alone was real; economy obeyed only its own laws and was determined by nothing outside itself. Everything else in human existence was merely a function of economy.[1]

Today we are convinced that this so-called materialistic or economic interpretation of history, as a generalization about culture, is false. We know that it is always spirit (*Geist*), as expressed in the Weltanschauung of the time, which gives form to a

---

[1] Translator's Note: The doctrine that we know in English as "economic determinism."

culture[1] and hence to an economic system. Even in a period when economy is dominant in the scale of cultural values, as it is in our age (which I have therefore called the Economic Age), we know that this economic primacy is the outgrowth of a particular Weltanschauung. Even though economy may also, in turn, affect the Weltanschauung men live by, the latter, nevertheless, remains primary.

A careful study of social relationships has taught us the truth of this and experience has confirmed it.

We can, however, best realize the influence of Weltanschauung upon economy by considering two different aspects of this influence: 1. the importance which economy has in the world of culture, or more exactly, in the world of values; 2. the interpretation of economy and its practice, the position of economy in the world of being.

I shall try to make these two aspects clear in the following sections.

II. The Evaluation of Economy

As we look over the history of mankind, we note that economy as a human end has been very differ-

---

[1] Translator's Note: The word *Kultur* I shall translate "culture." The German word, however, is not restricted merely to the artistic or aesthetic achievement of a people. "The list of all the items of the general life of a people represents that whole which we call its culture."—Webster.

Kultur also means the sum total of *human* achievement as opposed to *natural* occurrences; e.g., the distinction between the *cultural* sciences and the *natural* sciences, e.g., history and economics, as opposed to physics and chemistry. See pages 30 ff.

ently regarded at different times and in different places. In general we can differentiate three distinct conceptions of the value and significance of economy, each of which forms an age of history (although these eras do not necessarily follow one another).

I call them:

1. The Age of Magic
2. The Age of Politics
3. The Age of Economy

The Age of Magic covers all early civilizations. In the case of some peoples it lasted through their period of high culture, as in India and China. In this era ideas of magic controlled the imagination of men: they believed that nature had a soul; they believed that all human action—especially economic activity—must be directed toward influencing the supernatural world in favor of man, by means of magic. Hence the only reality in this age was this supernatural world, to which everything earthly— such as mere economy—was subordinate. Economy served religion, economy itself was religion (in the sense of cult); religion gave economy its form. Consumption was a religious act: cannibalism, taboo, dietary laws, the use of table luxuries, the wearing of ornaments, etc. Production also was religious: the division of labor between man and woman, the cultivation of land, the hunting of wild beasts, the taming of domestic animals. Everything economic in this era was looked on merely as a means of appeasing supernatural powers.

The Age of Politics is that era in which economy becomes a function of state policy. There are two periods in this era: the religious-political and the secular-political. The religious-political period comprises the early European state system, the Classical Age. At that time the religious and political spheres coincided. Spirits became gods and gods became holy guardians of the political community. At the same time religious aims came to be identified with state policy. Economy served this religio-political community. Only that economic activity which was of use to the state was permitted.

This political spirit, without religious consecration however, appeared again in the era of mercantilism, in the centuries of "modern times" when the absolute state was developing. Here, too, economy was a function of the state. Economy existed only to serve the interests of the state, which in this era were purely worldly.

At last began the Age of Economy, which is characterized by the primacy of economic interests. This era began in the western states of Europe in the eighteenth century and continues to this day in countries which still have a capitalistic culture.

I have recently, in my *Deutscher Sozialismus*,[1]

---

[1] Translator's Note: Translated under the title of "A New Social Philosophy," by K. F. Geiser, Princeton Press, 1937.

explained how widespread and how deep the influence of economic activity has been in those countries, so I shall not discuss the question again here.

If we have come to regard the present world situation as a critical one, it is because there are forces at work which are bringing our Age of Economy to an end. Economy will be unseated from the dominant position in our lives and made subordinate once more. It will have a meaning and a purpose beyond itself, an aim above the individualistic, materialistic interests which it has hitherto served.

This can occur, however, only if economy is organized on the basis of secular-political aims; secular, because of the fact that our dominant religion is Christianity, and Christianity cannot be made to play a positive, directing role in economy. Economy should be a servant member of the national community and the political commonwealth.

Economy has changed its form and become once again a branch of politics and this change is due to a change in Weltanschauung. Everywhere we notice the contrast to the liberalistic-pacifistic-individualistic standpoint which we used to hold. It is true that this reaction against the Economic Age in the different countries has been accompanied by very different ideas about other basic questions of existence, so that it is impossible to speak of a unified Weltanschauung in the anti-Liberal countries; for atheistic Bolshevism is just as anti-Liberal as the democratic Turkish system; idealistic Fascism is just as anti-Liberal as naturalistic National Socialism. But in each case we are concerned with an effect which Weltanschauung has had upon economy. This will become clearer still if we explain another connection between Weltanschauung and economy.

III. The Meaning of Economy

Besides the relation of Weltanschauung to economy that we have just discussed, which has to do with the evaluation of economy, there is another, which has to do with the meaning of the essence of economy. Whereas the question in the earlier discussion was the rank of economy in the world of values, in this section I shall take up the rank of economy in the world of being. In both cases it is a question of the antithesis of the Liberal and the anti-Liberal Weltanschauung; for this antithesis appears also in the different interpretations of economy in the world of being.

The Liberal theory of economics is the outgrowth of the Weltanschauung which was perfected in France and England in the eighteenth century and to which we can give the general name of Deism. The minds of the period were dominated by Isaac Newton's theory of the course of the stars, which held themselves in eternal equilibrium by attraction and repulsion and followed their courses in wonderful harmony. These physical concepts were transferred to human society and there was added the metaphysical concept of pre-established harmony according to which there are laws ordained by God for human society just as there are laws for the starry heavens. And it followed that, just as for the stars, the unhindered sway of these immutable laws would produce the greatest happiness and comfort for the individual and the community. This "natural order" was interpreted by the powerful class of men interested in the rising capitalistic system as meaning the free activity of individual business men. By the free play of the forces of attraction and repulsion, business men would produce a "harmony of interests" on earth, just as the heavenly bodies produce the "harmony of the spheres."

This faith in a harmonious economic order is based on the following beliefs:

1. The belief in "natural laws" for human society; that society is a natural formation; that spirit is only superficial.
2. The belief in determinism; that the will is part of the causality of nature.
3. The belief that man is by nature good—*le bon sauvage;* that man has been spoiled by the development of "civilization."

Opposed to this, anti-Liberalism has a different faith:

1. The belief in the spirituality of human society.
2. The belief in the spontaneity of the free will; that the will is responsible to itself alone.
3. The belief that man is by nature sinful.

From these two opposing Weltanschauungen we arrive at fundamentally different principles of economic policy. The belief that the human will is part of the natural process, that it is determined by the course of nature and that it is naturally good, leads to the demand for a Liberal economic order, which would have as few restrictions as possible. On the other hand, the belief in the free and by nature sinful will leads to normativism, that is, to an economic order conditioned by norms.

It is true here, as it was in the case of the different evaluations of economy, which I discussed above, that this part of a Weltanschauung can be combined with very different ideas on other parts of life. The demand for a normative economic system is accompanied by differing Weltanschauungen. Whether in the world of value or in the world of being, however, the new standpoint is determined by Weltanschauung.

CHAPTER TWO

WELTANSCHAUUNG AND SCIENCE

I. The Problem

UNLIKE the problem of the first chapter, when these two concepts are connected by the copulative "and," two questions arise:

What significance has science for Weltanschauung?

and

What significance has Weltanschauung for science?

I shall therefore divide this chapter correspondingly into two parts.

II. The Significance of Science for Weltanschauung

If we keep in mind the double meaning of the concept Weltanschauung, that it comprises on the one hand our ultimate ideas on life and, on the other, our ultimate values of life, we find that the significance of science for the creation of a Weltanschauung must be examined from this double point of view.

Concerning the first point, in modern times we have frequently been misled into believing that science itself leads to ultimate insight, that science can replace faith and metaphysics. According to the familiar scheme devised by the Comte de St. Simon, and later expanded by Auguste Comte, mankind is supposed to go through three phases: a religious, a metaphysical, and a scientific; and finally to remain for all time in the scientific.

Natural science in particular has been considered a substitute for both fundamental forms of transcendental knowledge. It was believed that natural science could aid in solving the riddle of the universe.

Today we see through this mental aberration. We know that science will never help us to discover "what really holds the universe together" *(was die Welt im Innersten zusammenhält* — Goethe)*.

What is known as a "scientific Weltanschauung" can justifiably have meaning only in the sense of agnosticism, only as a denial that a Weltanschauung can possibly have a non-empiric, "transcendental" basis.

This question does not concern us here, however, for our field of inquiry is economy and the science of economics. But the other question concerning the significance of science for Weltanschauung, namely, its significance as a basis for our ultimate values, is part of our main problem.

The question is this: do our values need a scientific basis and is such a basis possible?

The old Socratic question had been: can virtue be taught? And the Age of Enlightenment answered it

once again in the affirmative with the assertion that
values, and more particularly virtue, were objects of
scientific research and that hence their "rightness"
was "demonstrable." On this point the Age of Enlightenment found itself in agreement with rational-
istic scholasticism. And to this day we still feel the
influence of the old rationalism in all our cultural
sciences and by no means least in the science of economics. We are given to understand that it is the
duty of science to prove the rightness of values; but
values have by their very nature a transcendental
basis, since they invariably entail a judgment on the
meaning of human existence and this meaning can
be expressed only non-empirically in positive or
negative judgments.

The following is true of all "value judgments":
they comprise only "relatively" true knowledge;
relative, that is, to the knower. And no one can force
others by the processes of reason to believe in these
"truths." Values are envisioned by men of genius
and believed in by men of like mind. Values are
propagated—entirely irrationally—by the incalcula-
ble force of personality. Love replaces proof, and
emulation follows love. We live for values. We die
for values if need be. But we do not prove values.
What sense would it make to die for something that
you could "prove" to be "right"? The idea that
values can be proved right is only an old prejudice
of the Age of Enlightenment, which our economists

still share. To prove the "rightness" of values means compressing them within the narrow circumference of the understanding. It means trying to make science out of value-judgments. Values, however, have their basis beyond the reach of the plumb-line of science.

In the discussion about value judgments in economics, which has been usually very superficial, it should at last be realized that values, and hence judgments about values, lie outside the realm of empirical and evidential knowledge; in other words, outside what we traditionally call "science." Values belong to the sphere of philosophic (or religious) knowledge.

III. The Significance of Weltanschauung for Science

Our second main question leads us into a series of problems which belong to the so-called "sociology of knowledge" (*Wissenssoziologie*). The central problem in this field is the much discussed question of "relative knowledge" (*Standpunktwissen*). The questions are these: is there such a thing as knowledge without presuppositions, without conditions and limitations, or is all knowledge conditioned? And, if the latter is true, is knowledge conditioned in a natural sense, or in a *folkic* sense, or in a spiritual sense? Is knowledge necessarily conditioned, or not?

After prolonged study I have arrived at the following conclusions. There can be no doubt that we "know" from a definite point of view, that all human knowledge is conditioned, since it is obvious that knowledge is possible only to finite beings limited in space and time. This is true for the natural sciences as well as for the cultural sciences.

The standpoint of a person has a double foundation: 1. in his psycho-physical make-up, his "blood," and 2. in his values and knowledge, his spirit (*Geist*), which finds expression in his Weltanschauung.

The psycho-physical make-up of a person essentially determines his ability. It determines whether he thinks clearly or confusedly, whether he is equipped with the power of insight or the power of abstraction, whether or not he possesses a talent for form, and so forth. For example, other things being equal, the sharp Jewish intelligence of a Ricardo or a Marx would naturally produce a different economics from that produced by the "deep, German obscurity" (as Fichte called it) of an Adam Müller or a Knies or a Schmoller.

That knowledge is conditioned also by Weltanschauung, however, can be seen in the following:

1. The *purpose* of knowledge: knowledge can serve heavenly or earthly aims; in other words, its purpose can be to glorify God, to behold the power, wisdom, and goodness of God in all things; or its purpose can be purely mundane.

In its purpose, therefore, all modern science is conditioned; for science is the outgrowth of a particular Weltanschauung which has developed gradually since the decay of European culture at the end of the Middle Ages (about the thirteenth century) .[1] A critical, worldly spirit replaced the religio-churchly spirit. The center of interest turned from eternal values to the things of this world. There occurred, as I said above, a secularization of knowledge and of values, brought about mainly by the increase in wealth and the development of the city. At the same time there awoke an interest in the individual and in individualism and only after these changes was interest aroused in the problems which concern modern science.

But even within the sphere of modern science, which is as a whole conditioned, there are different purposes which can be explained only by the fact that science is conditioned by the Weltanschauung of the scientist.

Earthly knowledge can serve different purposes, either the purpose of knowledge itself, or some purpose outside itself. In the field of nature we can "know" in order to master nature, *savoir pour prévoir, calculer pour dominer*. In the field of culture, we can "know" in order to justify political or other practical demands or to acquire the means to better human existence.

---

[1] See page 4.

In modern Europe social science in particular has been chosen for this task. Very early in the history of social science the voice of the worthy J. J. Becher was heard protesting that science had no justification except in so far as it served "to correct the *statum corruptum* of humanity." And today the Socialists and Fascists call on science to assist them in their social struggles; they say that social science must "prove" the "rightness" of its main purpose or be condemned as mere empty theorizing.

Other social scientists, on the other hand, claim that even their science aims at pure knowledge.

2. We can see how Weltanschauung conditions science also in the *assumption of certain axioms* or articles of faith as the basis of knowledge. The scientist must have "faith," for example, either in a world system ordained by God, or in a "natural" world order, or in none at all. He is compelled to believe, if he wants to be a scientist at all, in the "fidelity of the world" (*Treue der Welt*) as the constancy of nature has been called. The scientist must believe that a cat will always be a cat and not suddenly a bird. He must even have the much more daring faith that the sun will rise tomorrow. And he must have a deep faith in the indestructibility of the categories of thought, in the evidence of *a priori* knowledge, in the "reasonableness" (*Vernünftigkeit*) of the human spirit.

3. A scientist's Weltanschauung conditions his

choices, whether it be a choice of problems, or of "organizing ideas" *(Arbeitsideen)*, or of method.

The choice of problems.—Ricardo made ground rent the central problem of his discussions, because as a fortunate stockholder he was especially interested in the reduction of the interest rate.

Sismondi studied in particular problems of markets and crises, because, as a *petit bourgeois,* he was depressed by the want of his Swiss home craftsmen.

Marx worked out the nature of big industry and the conditions of the wage workers, because he wished to create a basis for his theories of revolution.

In general, it can be said that the Liberal is interested mainly in the problems of trade, stock exchanges, money and market behavior (exchange rates, prices, etc.) ; the Marxist more in the nature of industry, the division of labor, the organization of the workers, the wage system and the distribution of income; the Nationalist more in the state of the farmer and the middle class and in the more general problems of production, state economic policy, autarchy, etc. Each of these standpoints emphasizes a different part of the economic process; the Liberal emphasizes turnover, the Marxist distribution, the Nationalist production.

The choice of organizing ideas.—By "organizing ideas" I mean concepts which enable us to organize the subject matter of economics within the framework created by basic ideas (*Grund- und Gestalt-ideen*). Organizing ideas therefore imply ways of looking at things, attitudes, ways of asking questions, "guides to observation" (Kant). There are many of them and—what interests us here—scientists choose them, often without being conscious of making a choice, each according to his own particular Weltanschauung. I shall try to make clear some of these organizing ideas.

Organism and mechanism are a pair of such concepts. Economic activity is thought of either as an organism, a creation possessing a life and growth of its own, and composed of living parts; or as a mechanism, an unchanging, artificial structure put together out of lifeless pieces. It is understandable that Nationalists prefer the idea of organism whereas Liberals prefer the idea of mechanism; both are equally justified as long as they remember that an economy is neither an organism nor a mechanism.

Another pair of organizing ideas are market society (*Marktgesellschaft*) and national economy (*Volkswirtschaft*).

The mercantilists, or Friedrich List, or the Fascists and National Socialists of today put the emphasis on the idea of national economy; and they do this because they wish, consciously or unconsciously, to bring greater power and glory to their nation and their people. On the other hand, the "classical" economists and their followers are interested in market and exchange conditions. Their point of view is so different because they are less interested in the fate of any one country and because they always think in terms of liberalism, individualism and pacifism. All those who believe in a national economy are "patriots." All "social economists" are "pacifists."

Let us finally look at the organizing idea, "value." It is significant that all economists who in their hearts are interested in preserving the capitalistic system believe in some psychological theory of value, particularly the marginal utility theory, because with the help of this theory they believe it can be proved that the capitalistic system is the best of all economic systems, indeed that its foundation rests in the very nature of economics itself. On the other hand, the opponents of the capitalistic system talk about the "labor theory of value," whether they wish to use it to prove the "injustice" of the present economic system, or whether, like Karl Marx, they wish to use it to deduce the inevitable collapse of capitalism.

The choice of method.—This also is influenced by Weltanschauung. All those scientists who believe that economics has laws peculiar to itself use an evolutionary or a "dialectic" method, whereas the opponents of this point of view prefer a voluntaristic attitude. I shall, however, leave the discussion of this point for the next chapter. For in this instance, the subject matter of economics—that is, the economic system current at the time—has a decisive influence, in turn, upon the nature of the science of economics itself.

Up to this point we have shown that in many cases science is conditioned by "blood" and by spirit, that 1. scientific study *can* be influenced by the personality of the scientist (and consciously or unconsciously *is*). But there are two more questions to be brought up and discussed before we can fully master the problem of whether and how science is conditioned. The additional questions are: 2. must science of necessity be guided by the personality of the scientist? And 3. (in so far as it does not need to be) should it be?

The second question, as to whether science is indissolubly bound to Weltanschauung or not, can be answered thus: a blood tie is indissoluble, a spiritual tie (e.g., a Weltanschauung) is soluble. For example, if I am stupid, I cannot become clever no matter how hard I try; but if I am a Saul, I can always become a Paul; if a Communist, I can always become a National Socialist.

The third question is this: in these cases where science is not indissolubly bound to the personality of the scientist, does the influence of Weltanschauung have any effect on scientific study; and if so, does it have a good effect or a bad one; and hence, should the tie between science and Weltanschauung be broken whenever possible?

The question can be answered thus: it is not harmful for science to be tied to Weltanschauung as long as the scientific conclusions are not affected. Wherever Weltanschauung affects scientific conclusions, however, the tie is harmful.

The standpoint, the Weltanschauung, of a scientist must never lead him to false conclusions. A scientific observation is correct or false and the "standpoint" of the scientist cannot change that. For example, if I state that the middle class came into being in the age of High Capitalism, the statement is equally true whether I am a Marxist and want to do away with the middle class, or a National Socialist and regard the middle class as the very center of a national economy. It is necessary only to recognize certain fundamental axioms, as I explained above. I cannot, for example, be engaged in science at all in the modern, western sense, if my Weltanschauung is based on magic. That, of course, is obvious.

For the rest, the scientist can think whatever he wishes and however he wishes about the world. We, as men of science, are entirely indifferent to the peculiarities of the scientist's Weltanschauung. For they do not harm scientific study. On the contrary, the influence of a strong Weltanschauung can often be of service to science, as the history of science, especially the science of economics, abundantly illustrates. For example, the faith of François Quesnay in the natural laws of economics gave us the *tableau économique.* The passionate patriotism of Friedrich List gave us the theory of productive forces. Karl Marx's fanatical hatred of the bourgeoisie disclosed to us the nature of capitalism. Even when the standpoint of the scientist is false, he can contribute, nevertheless, to science. His Weltanschauung guides him to important problems and his wish to realize certain ideals makes him clear-sighted and strengthens his will to get to the bottom of things. To the disinterested man the deepest truths remain a closed book. Only men with a passionate belief, with a passionate will can become great scientists.

But one thing can be demanded of every serious scientist: he must be guided in his work by no other thought than to know the truth. He must have no other interest but science, whether that other interest be his religion, his state or his people. Otherwise his work is valueless; valueless even for religion, state or people. That is no *l'art pour l'art* attitude; for it is not the duty of the scientist to fit science or art into the totality of state or culture.

In this connection I should like to quote Leopold von Ranke, who once said that science must dig deep into life, must leave its mark on current history; and he added, "But in order to have influence science must, above all, be science. There is only one way that we can leave a true impress on our times and that is to forget our times and raise ourselves to free, objective science."

Most dangerous of all is the attitude that has been called "reflexive nationalism," the attitude that the creative worker should strive to be as "national" as possible, that a German, for example, should be as German as possible. This attitude is the death of all creative activity. What would have happened to Dürer's paintings if with every stroke of the brush he had stopped to think, "will this be a German painting"?

This is true in all creative fields and by no means least in the field of economic studies. To wish to create a "German" economic theory, if we mean by that an economic theory for Germans, is an undertaking which is foredoomed to failure; or rather which will always bear the stamp of mediocrity. Whoever is a good German, will paint German pictures, compose German poems, think German thoughts, even when he is least conscious of being a German; in fact, precisely when he is not conscious of it. The important thing is self-dedication; for only then will creative work of value be done (if we assume that in addition to self-dedication there is also ability).

CHAPTER THREE

SCIENCE AND ECONOMY

I. An Error Corrected

BEFORE I attempt to outline the relation of science with economy, I must correct a strange error which is very often made. Economy (*Wirtschaft*) and the science of economics (*Wirtschaftswissenschaft*) are often mistaken for each other. Critics make this mistake frequently when they criticize doctrines they do not favor. They often attack the science of economics when they mean economy itself, as, for example, when critics of the present times complain of materialism, money-grubbing and calculativeness.

We find this confusion between economy and the science of economics even today among critics who are themselves trained economists. When we hear economics blamed for being merely a "science of international profit," we are inclined to think that the blame should be put on the economic system instead.

But, however that may be, we must always remember that economic science and an economic system are two different things, which of course have a connection, but which must not be confused with one another. It is obvious that the relation of these two concepts is not the same as the relationships we have already discussed, but since each has some effect on the other, I shall make the same division in this chapter as in the last.

II. The Significance of Economy for the Science of Economics

I shall mention only in passing the familiar fact that a certain type of economy—the capitalistic system—plus circumstances caused by that system, has brought about a special science of economics.

The problem I shall discuss at length in this section however is this: what demands do economy in general and certain historical systems in particular make upon a science of economics? Since, in my opinion, the subject matter of a science ought to determine the nature and practice of that science, the following discussion will be nothing less than a "methodology," or a theory of procedure in a nutshell, for the new economics. Let me refer those who wish a more thorough treatment of this subject to my book, *Die Drei Nationalökonomien* (1930), which bears the subtitle "The History and System of Economic Theory."

Here, however, I shall say this much. All economy, like all human culture (*Kultur*), is spirit (*Geist*). Therefore the science of economics must be a "spiritual" science (*Geistwissenschaft*). It has been the ill fortune not only of the science of economics but of almost all the cultural sciences that this fact was so long unrecognized; categories which have validity and usefulness in the natural sciences were taken over into the spiritual sphere. The result is that all post-mercantilist economic theory, from the French and English "classicists" and the historical school, down to the mathematical school and the marginal utility school have adopted the reasoning processes of the natural sciences, which, applied to economic science, are false. This science I have named "self-ordering" (*ordnende*) economic science.[1]

During all this time the science of economics was working toward the wrong aim of trying to find "laws" analogous to the laws of natural science, "regularities" derived from experience and expressed in neat formulas, by which particular "cases" could be classified.

---

[1] Translator's Note: The distinction between what the author calls *ordnende* science of economics and what he calls *verstehende* economics (see page 34) is the subject of discussion in the following pages and is basic to the philosophy of economics expressed in this book.

Ordnende, which means also "classifying," "regulating," I have translated "self-ordering." This older science of economics orders, classifies, regulates its subject matter according to generic and specific laws in the manner of natural science.

Verstehende (literally "understanding"), I have translated "cognitive." This new science of economics "understands," feels its subject matter directly and intuitively.

All believers in the old economics agreed also on the way to reach this goal of their science: reduce the economic picture to its elements, to the least common denominators, quantities possessing the fewest qualities. "Economics must go beyond the diversity of appearances in search of ever simpler elements. Economics strives toward absolute, simple points of departure. If these points were once discovered and fixed, then all existence could be scientifically derived from them." (Schmoller.) Such "atoms" of economics they found in "human desires," "instincts," in labor and the like.

General laws were set up by this process, laws like the law of labor costs, or the law of marginal utility and the like. From these general laws special laws were deduced like the law of wages, the law of rent, the law of interest rates and so on.

The general laws corresponded to the laws of mechanics, the special laws to those of physics.

This application of the thought processes of the natural sciences to economics has failed completely and for the following reasons:

1. The free will of man makes any ascertainment of regularity impossible.

2. The "matter," in which it was thought that regularity could be found, does not exist.

3. The spiritual facts which form the contents of all economy are complex and cannot be resolved into elemental parts.

But no such refutation is necessary if we remember that we can study the subject matter of the cultural sciences, the world of spirit *(Geist)*, *without* making a detour through natural science. Since all culture is spirit of our spirit, we are at home in this world, whereas we must ever remain foreign to the world of nature. We "understand" the world of culture, we have insight into the "sense" of it, we know it "inwardly."

The world of culture, and hence economy, we know with our cognitive faculty *(verstehen)*; the world of nature we can only apprehend *(begreifen)* intellectually and objectively because nature is foreign to our senses; and it is foreign to us because we did not create it. Our reactions to the phenomena of nature are very different from our reactions to the achievements of culture. If we compare a tree with a factory, a whirlwind with a stock market maneuver, the fall of leaves with a fall in prices, it becomes easy to distinguish the different standards of knowledge which we apply to the two fields, and to see that our higher knowledge of cultural things is attributable only to the fact that we ourselves have created them.

Therefore, we should understand *(verstehen)* economic life, we should grasp its "sense." We should not trouble ourselves to try, by means that are insufficient, to describe, measure and weigh economic data and then put down the results of our attempts (which we do not understand) in a few formulas which we call "laws"; for in the end these laws are of no use to us, since—as I explained above —we are in no position to "classify" individual "cases" under them.

It would be false, however, to conclude that "cognitive" (*verstehende*) science merely dissolves knowledge into a series of individual, perhaps differing, opinions and leads to an everchanging subjectivism, —an objection which many have made. Nor is it right to say that cognitive science has returned to sheer empiricism and rejected all objective laws and all "theory." Nothing could be more unfounded than this objection. Cognitive economic science understands thoroughly the idea of "laws" and appreciates the value of theory. These two concepts, however, have a somewhat different meaning from their meaning in the natural sciences and therefore they occupy a different position in the totality of knowledge.

We have seen that self-ordering (*ordnende*) economics uses the word "law" in the sense of a law of nature and understands obedience to laws as meaning a regularity deduced from experience. This regularity, however, must lack necessity since necessity can never be deduced from experience. These laws then are not genuine laws. On the other hand "cognitive" (*verstehende*) economics conceives laws once more in the original sense, as genuine laws, apodeictic judgments which have necessity. Therefore, since necessity cannot be derived from experience, genuine laws of the type that cognitive economics recognizes, must have *a priori* validity; that is, they must be based on thought-evidence (or intuition-evidence) .

There is no lack, therefore, of "economic laws" in cognitive economics, but these laws have a different structure and have an entirely different significance in the progress of knowledge from what they have in the self-ordering, natural science type of economics. The difference is this: laws in cognitive economics stand at the *beginning* of research, not at the *end*. They are not the aim of research but the means to realize the ultimate purpose of the "spiritual" science type of economics, which is to understand the nature and interrelationships of the economic process.

Cognitive economics has made a similar reversal in the relation of theory to empiricism.

I have already remarked that it is nonsense to claim that the new economics neglects theory or that it is pure empiricism. Such an opinion could come only from ignorance. Obviously the economists of the old school do not know what either theory or empiricism is. Let me then say once more: theory has to do with whatever can be thought and consists of three parts: the theory of possibilities, the theory of probabilities and the theory of necessities. On the other hand, empiricism has to do with actualities: it is knowledge of the particular, as opposed to the general, the knowledge of phenomena in space and time.

It is clear that a realistic science like economics must of necessity consist of a union of theory and empiricism. Therefore, to contrast "theoretical" with "historical" economics, or even "rational" with "empirical" economics is meaningless. Whoever does not practice both theory and empiricism is not a complete economist but only a part of one. He walks on one foot and not on two like a healthy man. There is a saying of Kant's which we can paraphrase to express relation between the two sides of our science: economics without theory is blind; economics without empiricism is empty. But I admit that our approach differs essentially from that of the old school in the proportion that we assign to each.

Here we must make clear that the science of economics has a double field of study. On the one hand, economic science must study the facts and relationships that are common to all economy; on the other hand, those that are applicable only to particular economic systems. Examples of the two different fields: goods and price; physical production and credit economy; management and capitalistic enterprise. These concepts exist on two different planes, so to speak. They belong to fundamentally different sense contexts; the first of each contrasting pair is applicable to all economy, the second to one particular economic system. The categories in terms of which we think of the first group are general-economic. The categories in terms of which we think of the second group are historical-economic.

It is false therefore to say, as so many do today, that all economic phenomena are historically conditioned. There are also universal economic phenomena, the study of which is an essential task of the science of economics. To name only a few: physical need, goods, productive factors, earnings, income, productivity, the interdependence of the parts of the economic process, wealth, etc.

But it is also false to call these general-economic categories a pure economic science (in contrast to a political economic science) and to make out of the study of these categories a "pure economy."[1] This idea of a pure economy is derived, characteristically enough, from the spirit of the natural science type of economics. It was believed that a "natural" economy existed, uninfluenced by contemporary society or by the political order. Wiskemann has rightly called it a "phantom"; for there is no such thing in reality as a "free," "natural," unregulated, non-political economy. The idea of economy, if it is to be conceived at all as a phenomenon of culture, necessarily

---

[1] Translator's Note: The phrase appears in English in the German text.

includes the idea of regulation, that is, the idea of human institutions, of which the order of the state is an essential part (provided that the state is properly conceived as being the largest political unit, which *always* exists) . In this sense—I repeat—all economy is, if it can be conceived at all, necessarily "political economy."

On the other hand, it remains true that the subject matter of economic science consists mostly of phenomena that are historically conditioned. It is one of the main tasks of the science of economics to understand the very particularity of these phenomena and to describe them. It was the great mistake of the old school to ignore the different types of economy, to recognize only one economy—the capitalist —and to consider that one alone as the "natural" economy. This misconception was the result of thinking in terms of natural science: just as there is but *one* nature, so there is but one economy.

Every good economics is an historical science without thereby being merely history. How it is possible to have an historical economics without its dissolving into the mere history of economic systems (that is, pure empiricism) , I have described sufficiently in my larger works and I shall not discuss it at length here. In this connection it is important only to remind ourselves once more how strongly practical economic life influences economic science; the bare fact that economic life is so diverse, proves—unless one is willing to shut out life entirely—the historical character of economic science.

And economic science is dependent on economic life in a further sense, in that its mode of knowledge and methods of research are conditioned by the historical forms of economic life. We saw above (pp. 19 ff.) that the methods of knowledge and research of our science were often under the influence of Weltanschauung, but we can see at this point that the influences of Weltanschauung are limited, if science is to be practiced in an objective manner: the mode of knowledge and the method of research are to a great extent prescribed by the type of economic system which is being studied.

I shall limit this broad problem to one question: what is the relation of the economic system to economic science in the economic system under which we live, namely, capitalism? It can be shown that capitalism, not only as a whole, but also in its three historical phases—Early, High and Late Capitalism, —makes special demands on the science of economics.

One section of my *Moderner Kapitalismus* (Vol. II, pp. 912-942) is entitled "The Economics of Early Capitalism." There I tried to show how perfectly "mercantilism," which is what we call the economic science of that period (from the end of the fifteenth century to the beginning of the nineteenth), was adapted to Early Capitalist economic life. I also discussed the contrast of mercantilist economics with the later economics under High Capitalism, in regard to their problems, methods, field of study and purpose of research. I came to the conclusion that the thought of the theoreticians of Early Capitalism was organic, dynamic, activistic, idealistic, concerned with problems of production; the thought of their successors under High Capitalism was mechanistic, static, materialistic, passivistic, concerned with problems of turnover. If I were writing today I would add a further important contrast: the mercantilists thought teleologically and their successors causally. In what way the mercantilist manner of thought was valid for the problems of Early Capitalism I have shown in the above-mentioned book.

It is also not difficult to show how the economics of High Capitalism was suited to the economic practice of its day. The period of High Capitalism was, as we know, characterized by the self-glorification of the economic life. And economic activity, which had formerly been concentrated in the halls of government or managed by the guildmasters or the responsible elders of the village, was transferred in this period to the offices of the business men. And these men, each with his own bare fists, and each with a clear conscience, started on the quest for profit. What could economic science do, faced with such a strange state of affairs, except to study the outcome of the battle? The sequence of events which required interpretation was very like the course of nature.

"Laws of the market" had to be discovered just as scientists had discovered laws of the spheres. Such a situation offered the self-ordering (*ordnende*), natural science type of economic science a rich field of inquiry. And if we ask why economic science was dominated for a whole century by the thought processes of the natural sciences, we can find—besides the influence of fashion—one of the reasons in the peculiar economic life of the time. It was all too tempting to apply the categories of natural science to the economic developments of the age of High Capitalism, developments which were in truth very similar to the processes of nature. Even cognitive (*verstehende*) economics would sometimes have had to use similar methods; even had it not looked for "natural" laws, it would, nevertheless, have had to fit its fictitious laws, its rational schemata to the peculiarities of a free economy. Even cognitive economics would have had to set up price laws, laws of business cycles, rent laws, laws of interest rates, laws of labor, etc.

But now the question arises: have not conditions changed? Have not essential characteristics of the economic picture been altered, so that the assumptions underlying the old kind of economic science no longer hold good?

We know that this is the case. After the War economic life found itself in a period of transition. In my terminology, the epoch of High Capitalism ended and the epoch of Late Capitalism began. A fundamentally controlled economic system has taken the place of an economic system which was fundamentally free.[1]

The conclusion that we must draw from this fact, so far as the science of economics is concerned, is this: in the same degree that economy loses its free trade character, the analogy to the physical sciences loses its meaning. The search for "laws," as rational schemata for the free occurrence of economic events (which was the main activity of the old "theory") no longer has any meaning. What is the purpose of schemata when they no longer correspond to the facts? What is the purpose of price or wage laws (schemata), when prices and wages are no longer left to develop by themselves, but are fixed? What is the purpose of a law of exchange rates when there is no longer a free exchange market, or the purpose of a theory of business cycles, when there no longer are any business cycles? What is the purpose of a law of ground rent in an age when farm estates can be transferred only by inheritance?[2]

It is here that the old school of economists showed their lack of historical sense. They did not realize that an economy and, to a great extent, an economic science exist in time. They did not see that there

---

[1] A detailed discussion can be found in my book, *Die Zukunft des Kapitalismus*, 1932.

[2] Translator's Note: A reference to the new farm inheritance law in Germany.

were events in economic history—for example, the expansion boom in the age of High Capitalism—which never had occurred before and which never would occur again. They could not see that even the "theory" of such events would have its day.

An example: anyone drawing charts of short, medium and long-term business fluctuations when there are no more fluctuations is like the man who still makes tests of the pulling power of horses long after horses have disappeared from the highways.

If we want to find fault with the old economists we should not, therefore, say of them that they have a bad moral character or an outmoded Weltanschauung, but simply that the set of tools they use is obsolete.

There must be a new economic science and, more particularly, a new economic theory simply because there is a new economy in the world.

The question of what kind of economic science will fit the changed situation brings us to the other problem concerning the relationship between economy and science and must be taken up in connection with that problem: namely, the significance of science for economy.

III. The Significance of the Science of Economics for Economy

I shall not, at this point, go into the question of the meaning of economic science in general. I shall merely say that I disagree with those who believe that science (and especially economic science) cannot and should not be an end in itself but must serve practical purposes only. I disagree for reasons of Weltanschauung, a kind of disagreement not subject to discussion.

On the other hand, it is certainly true that economic science should serve practical ends and the only question that comes up here is whether our science can do this and, if so, in what way.

In order to answer this question, we shall first have to clarify the situation and remove a great many errors and false judgments which have crept into the discussion of these problems.

The great mistake in these discussions has been that the relation of science to "practice," which is so effective in the natural sciences, was transferred much too literally to economic science. It has not been noticed how different the two fields are.

In the first place, practice has a very different meaning in economic science from what it has in the natural sciences. The "practitioners" of natural science are those who use technical inventions in their business. They are the manufacturers, the transporters, the producers in a broad sense, business men. In our field also, these same men are the "practitioners," as opposed to the "theoreticians"; and for them economic science is something that can be of use. But in economic science we have as practitioners, in addition to business men, also those engaged in political affairs, especially statesmen and state officials. "Practical" life, therefore, in our science comprises two fields of human activity.

In the second place, the relation between "theory" (in a further sense, in which it is the opposite of practice, not the opposite of empiricism) and practice is very different from their relation to one another in the natural sciences.

In both fields technology has its place between theory and practice: in natural science, there are countless "technologies"; in our field, there are the three familiar technologies:

1. The art of private business which is now called the science of management (*Betriebswissenschaft*).

2. The art of public economy, now known as the science of finance (*Finanzwissenschaft*).

3. The art of "practical" national economy (*praktische Volkswirtschaftslehre*).

The basic characteristics of technology are the same in both fields.

By technology we mean the study of the means by which a particular aim can be realized. Technology differs from all "normative" (philosophic) studies (although it has falsely been called a normative science), in that technology is not concerned with norms or aims, but only with the means for carrying out these aims; aims are prescribed *for* technology. Technology makes no value-judgments, except technological ones which are concerned with fitting particular means to particular ends. In that respect technology is like science. But it differs from science in the problems which it attempts to solve. Science searches for what *is*, whereas technology strives to find out what *must be done* if a particular aim is to be attained. Science teaches, if we may use a dangerous expression, theoretical knowledge; technology, practical knowledge. Our western neighbors express the distinction between science and technology, especially in economics, more sharply than we do and they have made the difference clearer by the names they give each field. One branch they call "science" and the other "art." [1] Science: the indicative; art: the imperative.

But in two respects the field of spirit-knowledge (*Geisterkennens*), which includes the subject of economics, is absolutely different from the field of nature-knowledge (*Naturerkennen*): namely, in the relation of science to technology and the relation of technology to practice.

The natural sciences, at least those like physics and chemistry that can be practically useful, set up rules (so-called "laws") which are binding for long periods and in all cases.

These "rules," which natural science sets up, are applied by technology to the treatment and process-

---

[1] Translator's Note: The words "science" and "art" appear in English in the German text.

ing of natural materials. That is, technology applies the general rule to the specific case. Technology can do this because the materials and forces with which it deals always remain constant. As soon as science discovered that chromules were contained in coal tar, dye chemistry invented a process by which all dyes could be produced from coal tar, and the chemical industry applies this process.

In the field of cultural knowledge, however, the relation of science, technology and technic, i.e., practice, to one another is entirely different. It is different for the obvious reason that when it comes to practical action the problems in the field of culture are so very different from the problems in the field of nature. In the world of nature, technic has to do only with known quantities. Even the most daring technical novelties,—such as wireless telegraphy, airship construction, or the reduction of nitrogen from the air—are possible only by applying known forces to known materials; indeed, the most exact and most thorough knowledge of these forces and materials is necessary. Where human relationships are concerned, on the other hand, known factors must be combined with unknown in order to achieve a desired effect. Those things are *known* which have been intellectualized, which have become cultural concepts; such are legal systems, moral codes, organizations of all kinds, tax systems, bookkeeping systems, statistics, rules and regulations, etc. That which is soul (*Seele*) is unknown. And that is, at times, a great deal.

Thus we can easily understand that science can never play the same role in the field of culture that natural science can in the field of the production of goods. In the field of culture, science can never set up rules which technology can follow; it can never be the natural foundation on which technology can be built up. And in the same way, technology can never develop for practice processes by which life can be ordered.

If we consider the peculiar situation in our field of inquiry, we must divide the problem of the relation between theory and practice into the following three questions:

1. Of what use is the technological study of business management to the business man?

2. Of what use is the technological science of finance or the art of practical national economy to the statesman and state official?

3. Of what use is the pure science of economics to technologists or to practical men, both business men and statesmen?

All three questions are much disputed. So far as the first and second are concerned, there are still to-day many business men, state officials and statesmen who look down on all "theoretical" education and would leave everything to "routine experience." That is certainly a false standpoint. For as private business and national economy become more and more complex, they cannot be administered without a systematic analysis and a thorough understanding of the subject. But that implies a "theoretic training" (in a technological sense). Obviously, this training must take into consideration the fact that times have changed. A few prophecies can be given here concerning the future forms of the study of economic technology.

The first of the three fields of economic technology, the science of business management, which has experienced a rebirth in the last generation, has become a study which will be very beneficial in the future. What must be done is to extend this science of management to all forms of economic life: on the one hand, to public and semi-public undertakings, which will play a larger and larger part in the economy of the future; and on the other hand, to agriculture and the handicrafts. But if it is to include these last named occupations, the entire basic principle of the science of management must be revised. Under the influence of capitalism it has become an art of profit making. The silent assumption is that every economic operation must be run on the profit principle; and to serve this principle all economic phenomena must be convertible into calculable quantities. One of the most important intellectual discoveries of this generation is that the profit calculus cannot be applied to all economic operations, or, even if it could be applied, that it should not.

In all calculation for profit there lies the danger

that certain branches of economic life which are culturally and spiritually valuable will be destroyed. The science of management must be developed further until it includes, especially for agriculture and the handicrafts, a theory of management which is not based on the profit calculus. That this is possible is shown by the accomplishments in these fields in earlier times.

Public economics has always received special attention, as being the most important single branch of economics. And the technology of this economics has a special name, the science of finance. This science, though there were signs of it in ancient times and in the Middle Ages, was developed most highly in the age of mercantilism, particularly in France. The attempt is often made today to create a genuine science of finance out of the technology of state finance. Well and good, so long as the technology of state finance, which is today so highly developed and so beneficial, is not tampered with.

It would be desirable if, along with the study of private business economics and the study of state finance, the practical study of national economy could take its proper place. This branch of the tree of economics is withered. We shall have great need in the future for trained economists (*Volkswirte*, as they are called these days). We shall need them more and more as our economic system changes from a "free" to a "controlled," or "planned" economy;

from a soulful (*seelsame*) to an intellectualized economy, from a competition economy to a management economy.[1] What we need today is a science of practical national economy, which will find the means to achieve a given purpose, which will solve problems of management in all fields of economy, and which will instruct our future officials and magistrates in their duties. In a word, what we need today is a new cameralistics.

The old cameralistics was developed, as we know, in the seventeenth and eighteenth centuries almost exclusively in Germany and Austria, and may be considered an especially German branch of economics. Cameralistics was a synthesis of all the practical measures and rules that were necessary for the management of state forests, public domain, state mines, state manufactories, etc. This is still today the subject matter of practical economics, as it is treated in the lectures and textbooks of German professors. But it has become a mere omnium-gatherum of all kinds of scientific and technological details, which have no dominant practical idea to unify them. A reformation of this science of practical national economy is an urgent necessity for the future.

It should be realized that this is a special subject

---

[1] Translator's Note: This is a reference to Germany; but the change is becoming noticeable also in "capitalistic" countries like England and America.

by itself which must not be confused with the science of economics. For all science, let me repeat, is in essence exclusively determined by theoretical ideas and must never be formed around a practical aim, whereas for technology the practical aim is the proper motivating force. In science the subject matter, system and method, are determined by the (theoretic) *terminus a quo;* in technology, by the (practical) *terminus ad quem.*

It seems to me there can be no doubt that the study of economics in the future will consist mainly of these technological, practical studies. All these technologies will have to be broadened and deepened. It will be through them that theoretical knowledge will affect practice.

There remains, then, only the last of the three questions to be answered: do the various economic technological studies need the *science* of economics for their progress and development and could this pure science of economics be of direct use even to the "practitioner"—to the business man or statesman?

A professor, especially if he is not familiar with the real situation, will be tempted to answer this question without hesitation in the affirmative. But it is not as simple as that. The fact is that in our field all our technological, practical studies have developed without any connection at all with the science of economics. And the science of economics has had no influence at all on practical life, whether in business or public administration. The science of economics did have a great period, at the turn of the nineteenth century, when it had a direct effect on practical life. When the forces of economic life, at that time chiefly capitalistic interests, were fighting for freedom from regulation, science "justified" their desire for *laissez-faire*. It was naturally easy to say: the government should do nothing. Science failed later, however, when it came to enacting positive measures of control. All these measures—from the laws for the protection of the worker to the stabilization of the mark —were carried out without scientific basis and even contrary to scientific theory.

In so far as economists have exercised a personal influence on political events, such as the influence exerted by the German academic socialists (*Kathedersozialisten*) on financial, commercial and social policy, it has not been because of their scientific ideas, but because of the weight of their ethical and political demands. The same is true of the enormous effect which Marxism had. This effect certainly cannot be traced to the scientific-economic principles which Marx propounded, but exclusively to his panacea-like philosophy of history with its strong leaning toward mysticism.

Is this involuntary asceticism which the science of economics practices based on the nature of things, or would it be possible for economic science, like natural science, to influence practical life?

From what has been said above it is clear that the science of economics can never play the same role as the natural sciences. I have pointed out that economics cannot set up rules according to which technology can be applied and practical men operate. Because this has been expected of it, the science of economics has been condemned to barrenness.

Nevertheless, the science of economics could well enrich the technological study of economics in a different way; it could even influence economic practice directly, surpassing natural science in that regard, for the natural sciences must always influence practical life through the medium of technology.

For this we need only think of the problems which confront a cognitive (*verstehende*) economics. As I see it, the questions are mainly these:

1. The science of economics must make men see the limitations of economics by showing the basic truths which hold good for all economy, whether private business or handicrafts; whether capitalism, Communism or National Socialism. It would be throwing out the baby with the bath, to carry historicism to extremes (as happens frequently today), and deny the existence of "eternal truths," *vérités de raison,* for economic life.

I shall put down here a few propositions which express such eternal truths of economics. "All economy consists of the economic attitude (*Wirtschafts-*

gesinnung), the economic order and technic." "Labor *and* nature are the sources of wealth." "By itself, additional labor power by no means implies an increase in wealth." "Over-population is a relative concept: it depends on three variables, number of people, productivity, mode of living." "The amount of wealth is determined by the volume of raw materials." "The wealth of a country must decline if worn out instruments of production are not replaced in like amounts and kind." "Capital can be formed only by savings or by the creation of credit." "The size of an industry and the degree of specialization between industries or within one industry are dependent on the extent of the market." "Unemployment can be abolished only by additional work, which, in turn, presupposes additional demand." "A country can pay its debts, in the long run, only in goods." The list could be extended indefinitely.

2. The science of economics should make clear the "here and now" of the economic situation of a country by systematically ordering the facts of economic activity, i.e., by studying from the scientific point of view, the material that is brought out by statistics, inquiries, etc. In so far as the science of economics is engaged in this work, it is economic research (*Wirtschaftskunde*), economic "sociography," the history of economics.

3. In order that the science of economics can fulfill its function, it must state the point of view

according to which its material is to be ordered, so that the subject will be clearly understood. The science of economics can accomplish this by working out a system of categories in terms of which all the historical forms of economy must be considered. In so far as economic science does this, it is the sociology of economics. A great deal of my life work has been devoted to the task of evolving just such an historical theory of categories for economic knowledge, and in working out this theory I have recognized the idea of the *economic system* as the most appropriate leading idea. The idea is this:[1] the economic system is a mode of economic activity which appears as a significant unit, within which each basic element of economy—the economic attitude, the economic order, technic—exhibits its particular form. So far, I have heard of no better principle of classification than this idea of the economic system. If a better proposal were made, I should accept it. It is important to state, however, that without some such formative idea as I have named, all judgments about historical realities are empty talk and mere nonscientific knowledge. In my *Ordnung des Wirtschaftslebens,* I have tried to show that the idea of a national economy (*Volkswirtschaft*), though it serves very well as an organizing idea (*Arbeitsidee*), cannot be used as a formative idea.

---

[1] A thorough discussion can be found in my book *Die Ordnung des Wirtschaftslebens.* 2nd ed. 1927, p. 14.

CONCLUSION

THE opinions which I have expressed here, though they contain the economic principles of the future, are not new. I have expressed them in speeches and writing for many years and in 1930 worked them out systematically and in detail in my book *Die Drei Nationalökonomien,* to which I have often referred in this essay.

What then, in the light of my ideas, is the state of economic theory in Germany today?

Fortunately, there is obvious on all sides a commendable will to construct a new economics, or national economic theory, which will correspond to the changed conditions. The main ideas of this reform movement also are good: namely, that all science should be close to living reality, that the people as a whole must be the center of consideration, that all economics is "political" and that economic theory must take account of that fact. Commendable also are a great many distinguished achievements in the various branches of economic technology. There come to mind the recent works of such men as Reitlinger, Halm, Zorn, Reiner, and interesting material in such magazines as *Der deutsche Volkswirt, Der deutsche Ökonomist, Währung und Wirtschaft, Die deutsche Handelswarte, Die Zeitschrift für Wirtschaftskunde,* etc., and the literature on the Four Year Plan.

One gets the impression that the new "cameralistics" is on its way.

Much less commendable, however, are all the writings—with a very few laudable exceptions—that attempt to lay down basic principles for a new *science* of economics or even to seek an epistemological basis for the "new" standpoint. The intentions of these writers are obviously the very best; their main point, the abandonment of the old "Liberal" theory, is certainly excellent. When I read their writings, however, I often have the impression that the leaders of the "new direction" lack complete insight into the problems of their subject. They are not quite sure of the main point. They do not know what the old Liberal theory really was, or what it led to, or wherein the old and the new science of economics really differ. For it should be clear that the difference does not lie in the "approach," as is so often stated today. Men of action (in business, for example) can differ in their approach, but not men of learning. For the latter the important things are the principles and methods which they use to master their subject.

The situation often stands thus: the young men are right, but they cannot prove it, for they lack a thorough philosophic training and education, which cannot be replaced by the strongest will or the most ardent enthusiasm.

Perhaps in itself this would not be so bad; perhaps we should say: let us wait and see!

"Wenn sich der Most auch ganz absurd gebärdet,
Es gibt zuletzt doch noch 'nen Wein."

("No matter how absurdly the must behaves, in the end it will nevertheless become wine.") But we cannot wait.

While the younger generation is aimlessly running about, the enemy is lying in ambush, ready at any minute to reconquer the battlefield which he has about lost today. This enemy, however, is the "old" economics; and the older men, in contrast to the younger, have at their command a well-tested intellectual training and a strict method. In fact, we are witnessing in Germany today the strange spectacle of the old Liberal economics, long pronounced dead, intruding once more with its law-making and schematizations, its obsolete learning disguised in a new dress. And all this entirely escapes the attention of the new direction.

There is no way to ward off this threatening danger except for our young men to study their science very diligently. And science is (I wish to disclose) a very difficult craft, just as difficult as that of a locksmith, or a cabinet-maker, and it must be studied earnestly and long.

CONCLUSION

The scientist must be just as enthusiastic *about* his work as the metal-worker or the cabinet-maker is about his. But *at* his work, he must not be carried away by enthusiasm, for it is likely to do harm by dulling his clarity of judgment. In science, only a cool head, a keen understanding and a methodical training can be of service. All science is "rational," or it is not science.

One of the first steps in this course of study is the comprehension of the problems involved. The object of this essay is to introduce this first step and it is hence dedicated to the youth of today and tomorrow.